Their Names Will Live On

written by Carey King

**McGraw-Hill
School Division**

New York   Farmington

This is the tale of a wall. It is a wall that crowds of people come to see. It is called the Vietnam Memorial.

The tale began when two people found they felt the same about something. One of them was a woman called Maya Lin. She is an artist.

Jan Scruggs was part of the tale, too. He was a soldier.

Scruggs had been in a war.

It was in a faraway land named

Vietnam.

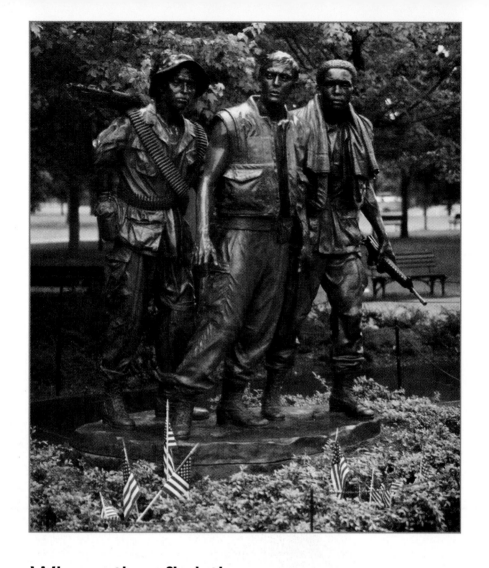

When the fighting was over,
Scruggs came home. But 58,000
men and women did not come
home to America.
Many had been killed in the
fighting.

"They were brave," Scruggs said. "We must not stop thinking about them." He wanted to do something to keep their names in people's minds. But what should he do?

Lin had a plan. She would make a wall. It would be made out of black stone. It would stand in a spot where everyone could stop and see it. She would sculpt the names of those who had been killed.

Scruggs liked the plan.

Scruggs and Lin went to

Washington, D.C., to get a

good spot for everyone to see.

"We need to save up to pay for this plan," said Scruggs. "We must speak out for help." Many people did help. Boys and girls gave coins, too.

Now they could begin the job.

Workers dug up the ground.

Many people came to see them.

Everyone who came spoke of someone who had been hurt or killed in the fighting.

Mothers, fathers, sisters, and brothers came. Boys and girls came to see the spot. Men and women on horses helped to keep things safe until everything was done.

The job was finished in 1982. All
the names of these brave people
were on the big stone. Now it is
seen by many people. The artist
is very proud of the fine work
she did.

Many people put things like notes, roses, and toys at the spot. They sit on the ground and chat. They read the names. Sometimes they cry.

It is a fine spot to think about
the brave men and women.